W9-CGQ-568

Printed in Hong Kong.
ISBN 0–89471–783–9.
Cover design by Toby Schmidt.
Interior design by Liz Vogdes.
This book may be ordered directly from the
publisher. Please add $2.50 for postage and
handling. *But try your bookstore first!*
Running Press Book Publishers
125 South Twenty-second Street
Philadelphia, Pennsylvania 19103–4399.

A Traveler's Diary

RUNNING PRESS
PHILADELPHIA · LONDON

From whatever place I write you will expect that part of my 'Travels' will consist of excursions in my own mind.

—*S.T. COLERIDGE* (1772–1834)
English writer

The Soul
of a journey is liberty, perfect
liberty, to think, feel, do just
as one pleases.

—WILLIAM HAZLITT (1778–1830)
English writer

A journey is
a person in itself; no two are
alike. And all plans, safe-
guards, policies and coercion
are fruitless. We find after years
of struggle that we do not take
a trip; a trip takes us.

—JOHN STEINBECK (1902–1968)
American author

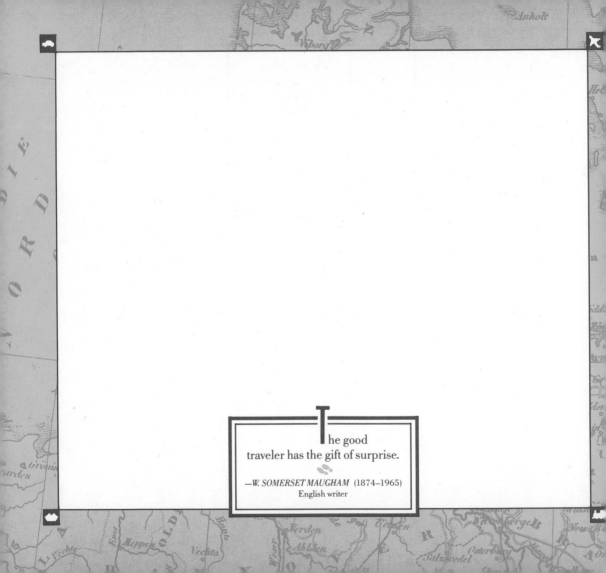

The good
traveler has the gift of surprise.

—W. SOMERSET MAUGHAM (1874–1965)
English writer

Travel is fatal
to prejudice, bigotry, and
narrow-mindedness.

—*MARK TWAIN* (1835–1910)
American author

Attitude,
speech, and clothes differ as
much from New York to Peoria
as they do from Chicago to
London.

—GAIL RUBIN BERENY, b. 1942
American writer

Is there anything as horrible as starting on a trip? Once you're off, that's all right, but the last moments are earthquake and convulsion, and the feeling that you are a snail being pulled off your rock.

—ANNE MORROW LINDBERGH, b. 1906
American writer

I hoped that
the trip would be the best of all
journeys: a journey into
ourselves.

—*SHIRLEY MACLAINE*, b. 1934
American actress

A traveler is
to be reverenced as such. His
profession is the best symbol of
our life. Going from—toward;
it is the history of
every one of us.

—*HENRY DAVID THOREAU* (1817–1862)
American essayist

*S*ome of them seemed possessed of an incorrigible inner urge simply to take off and explore, to use whatever excuse was necessary to travel into country where no one else had been, to see where the rivers went, to find a pass through a mountain range that no one else had crossed.

—*DAVID THOMPSON*, b. 1938
American writer

Keeping to the
main road is easy, but people
love to be sidetracked.

—LAO TZU (570 B.C.–490 B.C.)
Chinese philosopher

I think there is a fatality in it—I seldom go to the place I set out for.

—*LAURENCE STERNE* (1713–1768)
English writer

The traveler was active: he went strenuously in search of people, of adventure, of experience. The tourist is passive: he expects interesting things to happen to him. He goes "sight-seeing."

—*DANIEL J. BOORSTIN*, b. 1919
American writer

Traveling in
the company of those we love is
home in motion.

—LEIGH HUNT (1784–1859)
English writer

It is better
to wear out one's shoes than
one's sheets.

—*GENOESE PROVERB*

Never journey without something to eat in your pocket. If only to throw to dogs when attacked by them.

—E.S. BATES (1879–1939)
American writer

> **G**ood company
> in a journey makes the way
> seem the shorter.
>
> *—IZAAK WALTON* (1593–1683)
> English biographer

It is better
to travel alone than with
a bad companion.

—SENEGALESE PROVERB

> *S*omeone said to Socrates that a certain man had grown no better by his travels. "I should think not," he said; "he took himself along with him."
>
> —*MICHEL DE MONTAIGNE* (1533–1592)
> French writer

I never travel without my diary. One should always have something sensational to read in the train.

—OSCAR WILDE (1856–1900)
Irish playwright

A travel
adventure has no substitute.
It is the ultimate experience,
your one big opportunity
for flair.

—*ROSALIND MASSOW*, b. 1948
American writer

For some
ill-defined reason, lovers
have a particular penchant for
travelling, perhaps in the hope
that by exchanging backdrops
for that of the unknown, those
fleeting dreams will be
retained a little longer.

—*CAROLE CHESTER*
20th-century English writer

... The little
festive atmosphere of strange-
ness, of excitement, that only
a holiday bedroom brings.
This is ours for the moment,
but no more. While we are in it
we bring it life. When we have
gone it no longer exists, it
fades into anonymity.

—*DAPHNE DU MAURIER* (1907–1989)
English writer

Throughout history it has been man who worships and polishes the vehicle, and woman who packs the suitcases.

—JOHN FOWLES, b. 1926
English writer

Women have always yearned for faraway places. It was no accident that a woman financed the first package tour of the New World, and you can bet Isabella would have taken the trip herself, only Ferdinand wouldn't let her go.

—*ROSLYN FRIEDMAN*, b. 1924
American writer

Too often
travel, instead of broadening
the mind, merely lengthens
the conversation.

❧

—ELIZABETH DREW, b. 1935
American writer

Remember:
don't start conversations with
strangers on a trip. No way of
getting rid of them later!

❦

—*ISIDORA AGUIRRE*, b. 1922
Chilean playwright

Travelling and
freedom are perfect partners
and offer an opportunity to
grow in new dimensions.

—DONNA GOLDFEIN, b. 1933
American writer

Travelling
may be. . . an experience
we shall always remember, or
an experience which, alas,
we shall never forget.

—J. GORDON (1896–1952)
English writer

All saints can do miracles, but few of them can keep a hotel.

❧

—MARK TWAIN (1835–1910)
American writer

Don't confuse
your travel agent with God.

—KENNETH R. MORGAN, b. 1916
American writer

$$\mathbf{O}\text{ne always}$$
begins to forgive a place
as soon as it's left behind.

—CHARLES DICKENS (1812–1870)
English writer

People travel
to faraway places to watch, in
fascination, the kind of people
they ignore at home.

—*DAGOBERT D. RUNES* (1902–1982)
American writer

To look, really look out upon the world as it is framed in the window of a moving vehicle is to become a child again.

—ANONYMOUS

I was once
asked if I'd like to meet the
president of a certain country.
I said, "No. But I'd love to
meet some sheepherders."
The sheepherders, farmers
and taxi drivers are often
the most fascinating
people.

—*JAMES MICHENER*, b. 1907
American author

The traveler
sees what he sees; the tripper
sees what he has come to see.

—*G.K. CHESTERTON* (1874–1936)
English writer

I am sure
that no traveler seeing things
through author's spectacles
can see them as they
are. . . .

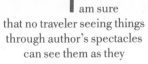

—*HARRIET MARTINEAU* (1802–1876)
English writer

The next best
thing to being rich is travelling
as though you were.

—*STEPHEN BIRNBAUM*, b. 1937
American editor and writer

" 'Go West,' said
Horace Greeley, but my slogan
is 'Go Anyplace.' "

—*RICHARD BISSELL* (1913–1977)
American writer

There are
three wants which can never be
satisfied: that of the rich,
who wants something more;
that of the sick, who wants
something different; and that
of the traveller, who says
"Anywhere but here."

—*RALPH WALDO EMERSON* (1803–1882)
American essayist and writer

Road, n.
A strip of land over which
one may pass from where it is
too tiresome to be to where
it is too futile to go.

—*AMBROSE BIERCE* (1842–1914)
American writer

Everything
in life is somewhere else, and
you get there in a car.

—E.B. WHITE (1899–1985)
American writer

Though a plane
is not the ideal place to really
think, to reassess or reevaluate
things, it is a great place to
have the illusion of doing so,
and often the illusion
will suffice.

—SHANA ALEXANDER, b. 1925
American journalist

Methods
of locomotion have improved
greatly in recent years,
but places to go remain
about the same.

—*DON HEROLD* (1905–1960)
American writer

Those who go overseas find a change of climate, not a change of soul.

—*HORACE* (65 B.C.–8 B.C.)
Roman poet and satirist

The wise man
travels to discover himself.

—JAMES RUSSELL LOWELL (1819–1891)
American poet

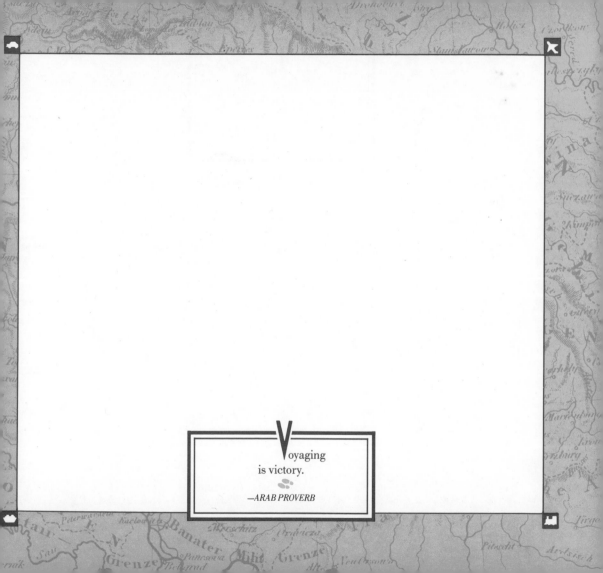

Voyaging
is victory.

—ARAB PROVERB

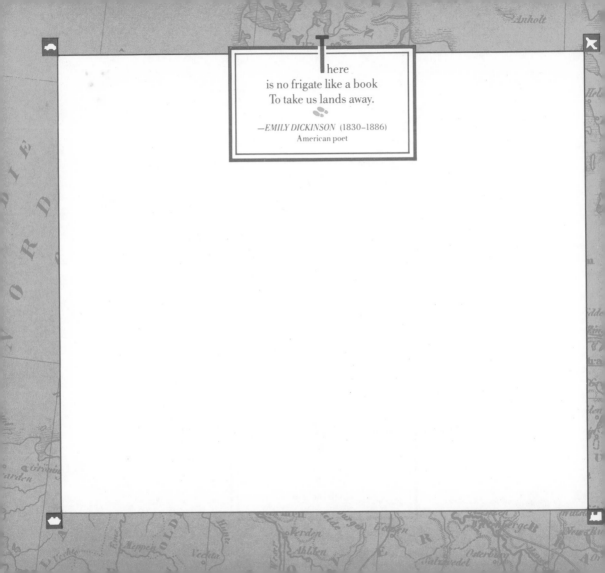

There
is no frigate like a book
To take us lands away.

—*EMILY DICKINSON* (1830–1886)
American poet

On a
long journey even a straw
weighs heavy.

—*SPANISH PROVERB*

It has been
my belief that in times of great
stress, such as a four day
vacation, the thin veneer
of family unity wears off
almost at once, and we
are revealed in our
true personalities.

—SHIRLEY JACKSON (1920–1965)
American writer

There are
two kinds of travel—first class
and with children.

—ROBERT BENCHLEY (1899–1945)
American humorist

Mileage
craziness is a serious condition
that exists in many forms. It can
hit unsuspecting travelers while
driving cars, motorcycles,
riding in planes, crossing the
country on bicycles or on foot.
The symptoms may lead to
obsessively placing more
importance on how many miles
are traveled than on the real
reason for traveling.

—PETER JENKINS, b. 1951
American writer

The border means more than a customs house, a passport officer, a man with a gun. Over there everything is going to be different; life is never going to be quite the same again after your passport has been stamped.

—*GRAHAM GREENE*, b. 1904
English writer

A good walker
leaves no tracks.

❧

—LAO TZU (570 B.C.–490 B.C.)
Chinese philosopher

Every land
has its own special rhythm,
and unless the traveler takes
the time to learn the rhythm,
he or she will remain an
outsider there always.

—JULIETTE DE BAIRCLI LEVY, b. 1937
English writer

A wise traveler
never despises his own country.

—*CARLO GOLDONI* (1707–1793)
Italian dramatist

"What place would you advise me to visit now?" he asked. "The planet Earth," replied the geographer. "It has a good reputation."

—ANTOINE DE SAINT EXUPÉRY
(1900–1944)
French author

It is a strange thing to come home. While yet on the journey, you cannot at all realize how strange it will be.

—*SELMA LAGERLÖF* (1858–1940)
Swedish writer (Nobel Winner)

Here I am,
safely returned over those
peaks from a journey far more
beautiful and strange than
anything I had hoped for or
imagined—how is it that
this safe return brings
such regret?

—PETER MATTHIESSEN, b. 1927
American writer

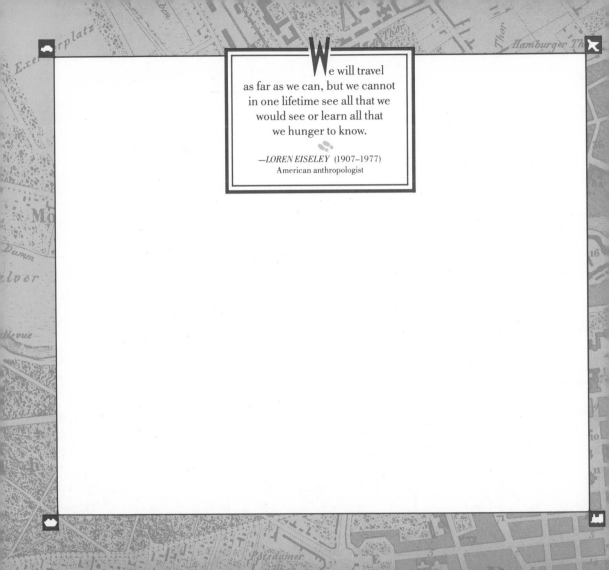

We will travel as far as we can, but we cannot in one lifetime see all that we would see or learn all that we hunger to know.

—*LOREN EISELEY* (1907–1977)
American anthropologist

We shall not
cease from exploration and the
end of all our exploring will be
to arrive where we started
and know the place
for the first time.

—*T.S. ELIOT* (1888–1965)
American-born English poet